Max Ellison

Double Take

Double Take

A Collection of Poems by
Max Ellison

Introducing the Poetry of
Lynn Berry

published by

CONWAY HOUSE
Conway, Michigan 49722

Foreword

Someone once said that to publish a book of poems was like dropping a rose petal in the Grand Canyon and then sitting back to wait for the echo.

I have found the response to poetry among the American youth much stronger than that. There is hardly a school where I visited but what some student or students ask me to read what they have written.

In one such school in New Jersey I met Lynn Berry teaching art in a junior high school, but filling notebook after notebook with poems that carried with them all the spectrums of emotion until I thought the pages should be damp with tears or sparkle with the sheer joy of youth. Needless to say, I asked Lynn to go with me on this trip.

In August of 1972 we spent a week picking out the poems we would use. Lynn picked the title, *Double Take*. Tim Hannert, the photographer, came up with the idea of the superimposed picture. Our friend and business associate, Art Anthony, ably helped us with the design of the book.

Had it all been left to me, I would have put the inside dust jacket picture on the front cover, and the title would have read *Listen to the Lynn*.

Max Ellison

Illustrated by
Lynn Berry

Photography by Timothy Hannert

Dedicated

to

Dr. George Gonzalez

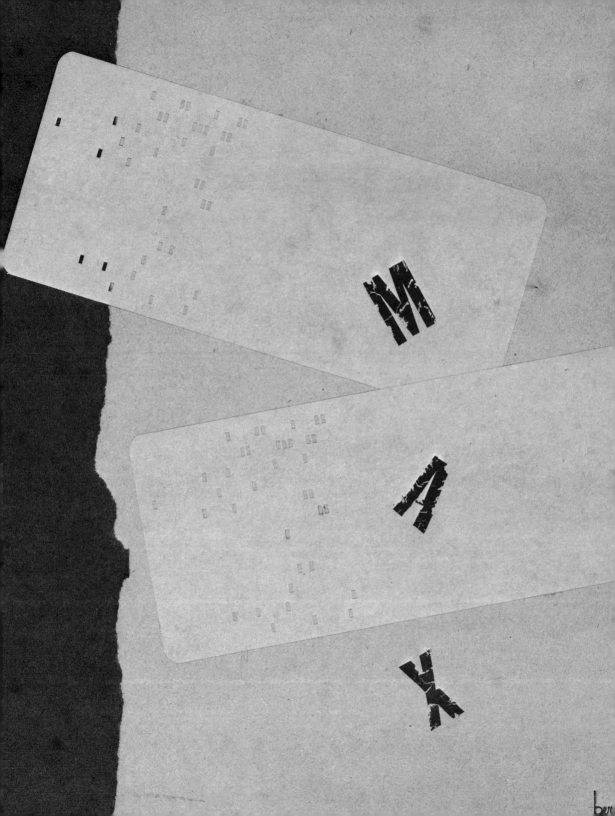

AN AUTOBIOGRAPHY

B.D.:	3-21-1914 A.D.
B.T.:	A
A.S.N.:	36422346
S.S.N.:	332-03-9660
Z.C.:	49722
A.C.:	616
Ph.:	347-2570
D.L.:	E. 425-593-585-229
C.A.:	74-571-724

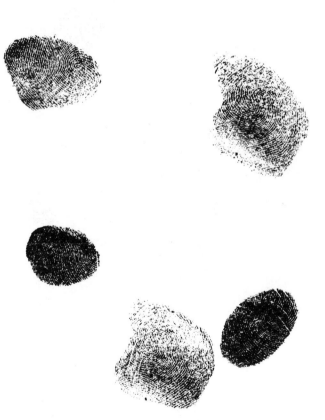

I have learned
That there is more
To being alive
Than pin pricks and deep breaths,
Just as
There is more to
Copping out
Than falling asleep;
But I always knew
That there was
More to crying
Than tears.

I hardly knew when dawn came;
First the outline of a street
With a house creeping out
Of the thin night,
Not unlike someone still sleeping
To whom silence was important
And slowness was the style,
With the town clock striking some hour
Shattering silence for at least a mile.

Picture yourself a poet
Too sensitive even to write.
Picture yourself dead, experiencing
All of life's beauty,
>   *and love,*
>   *and hope,*
>   *and friendship*
As time does not wait,
And you remain a spectator
At your own performance of life.

Lieing on my desk
In a gunmetal case
With the dust of Hialeah
On it's window-less face,
The commodity it worked with
Has dealt it a blow
So it no longer tells me
What I don't want to know.
It has no hands to wave,
No ticker that ticks.
It's wheels are not turning.
It's past being sick.
The one thing I'm sure of,
Its knotted string fob
Has tied it to nothing,
Neither time nor to God.

April 1, 1972
Petoskey, Michigan

Thoughts can only exist as such
    When they belong to one mind.
    If a thought is released,
    It is no longer a thought
    But a cheap conversation piece.
We should not confuse thought with gossip.

I reside in a field of thoughts;
    Sometimes there is a deep fog.
    Other times the sun falls on my field
    And makes it crystal clear,
And no one else can touch or it will break!

I have heard the silvery note from dawn's trumpet
Blowing a reveille for my heart,
Telling me to leave these grey mists and broken thoughts
That worldly dreams are composed of,
To walk on the high winds of the morning.

Recorded live
Was the sound of today,
Because I have just learned
That one cannot play
A stereo personality
On a monaural existence,
And this
Has weakened my hopes
Of a number one song.

KOOKY CREEK

Once on a mountain road I watched
A stream that seemed to be flowing uphill.
I was told that the laws of gravity were
As good there as they were at home.
It was only the angle of the mountain
That made my vision play this trick on me.

Being a guest and a stranger,
I accepted the explanation.
There was no choice, because
No choice was offered — but,
I have always suspected that the stream
Never reached the sea.

On the shores
Of the Ponchartrain,
I found that
A six pack of warm beer
Gives me a headache,
And seeing old friends
Is like blowing up a balloon
That already has a hole in it.

At Cape Hatteras I found out
My heart was just a gadabout.
I was beached, but it was free
To surf the waves, roam the sea,
And ride on ships, taste the storm,
See the weather being born.
I was on land and bound to stay,
But my heart became a stowaway.

March 5, 1972
Staunton, Virginia

Louisiana

Surrounded by
Bayou swamp,
Crowned with
Hanging moss,
I realized
That I was really
Not far
From home.

SAN FRANCISCO

I saw her as one bright star on the horizon,
Then from the sea, a million specks of light
To greet a tired careworn soldier
Coming from the blackness of the night.

San Francisco

Driving down
Stanyan Street
Made me wonder
If I could have
Written a better poem
    Myself?
And around the next bend
A voice
Cried out
Through the fog
Over the Golden Gate
And said . . .
"Do you realize how far
Away from home you are?"

What if God decided to drain the ocean?
He could if he took the notion,
And put the water some place else.
He would be the one to know how.
Not me. I couldn't even suggest.
The only place I know to keep oceans
Is exactly where they be.

Anyway, just think —
A thousand new mountain ranges.
And not only that —
Mountains with ships hanging from their side,
And chartered bus rides down rocky canyons
To look for gold coins that once knew the Spanish Main,
And signs all over the place saying,
"See the wreck of the Titanic — two bucks"
Or "She went down here,"
With ten motels at the foot of each mountain,
And a freeway so you could drive through
Without seeing it and exit here for
South Sea, No water — gas, food and lodging.
Stop at the Pequod Inn.

May God never do it. But,
If he did, someone would make a million,
And it wouldn't take us long
To louse it up.

March 15, 1971
Conrad, South Carolina

I dared to think
That I was
God enough
To paint a sunset.

Florence comes. Florence goes.
Where she is I do not know.
I heard water down the drain,
The screech of brakes, might be in pain.
If I go outside and seek,
I might find her in the street.
Might be in some lover's bed.
For all I know, she might be dead.
Florence is like the wind, you know.
First North, then South she comes and goes.
Pardon, while I shed a tear,
And announce to you, she is not here.

OLD GOATS

My eyes have grown a little dim.
My hearing's just a little thick.
And when I take a walk of late,
I sort of travel with a stick.
But I'm not old.

Things that happen now and then
Recall I've bettered two score ten,
Little things like the goat —
The old goat.

I saw it first against a tree.
I said a goat, but I could see
It wasn't that. It took the shape,
The form, the hew of some old goat.

But I knew, and checked my speed,
That someone with a need for art
Had found a stump, at least a part,
That took the form of a goat-like beast.

Against the trunk of tree he placed
This root-like mass with the goat-like face.
And I smiled as I sped on my way,
And whispered, "Old Goat," through the day.

For three days straight each time I passed
I slacked my speed and rolled the glass
To have a little closer look
At this goat-form the stump's root took.

I thought of how this tangled mass
Would fool most people as they pass
Into believing it was a goat —
An old goat.

The fourth morning it was gone.
I looked at noon, but could not see
A form against the front yard tree.
? — ? — ? — ? — ? — ? — ? — ?

I looked for clues and partly guessed —
The trashman — trashman — yes, that's it.
The trashman passed here yesterday.
He must have hauled the thing away.

I said, "Thing", and made a note.
Could I be wrong? — ?
Was it a goat?

berry

I looked it up in the dictionary:
  gobiet
  goblin
  go cart
  god
  god
  god

Like Harbor Memories

I'll be passing through
Every now and then
With the wind,
But I may dampen your window
Like the misty Newport fog
And be harder to get rid of
Than the smell of freshly killed salmon.

Written outside the study of Robert Frost
Ripton, Vermont, May 10, 1971

Inside,
There must be a chair and table,
And, with the curtain drawn,
He would be able to look down
On the walled meadows of his hillside farm
To see his house, his trees,
And the mountains beyond;
To hear the same bees I hear,
Or at least their kin,
Not busy with honey,
But trying to get in where I suspect
They have their grub-like brood.
And in this mood,
I see the chair —
I see the table —
And I am able to make my mind say, "This
Is the Anniversary Day of words he wrote."
It had to be May.
Beautiful words, I recall,
About a neighbor — some stones —
And the mending of a wall.

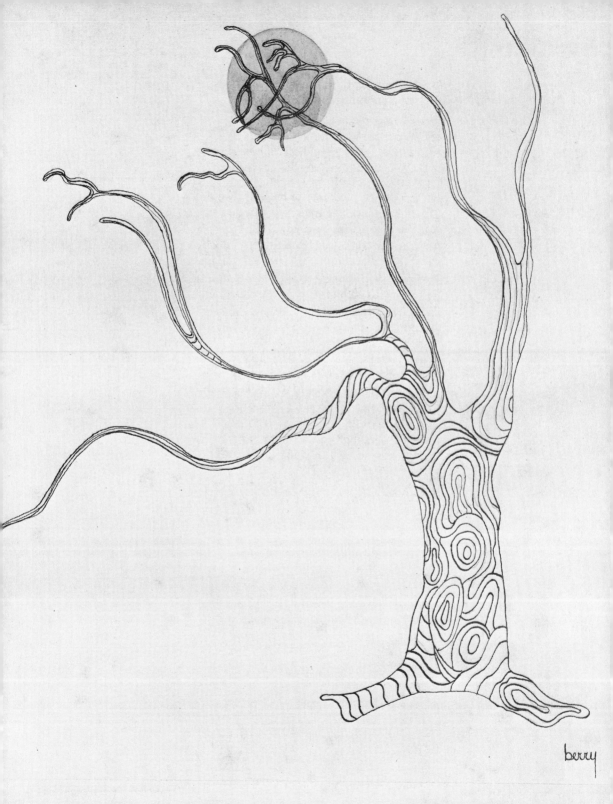

berry

"John Brown's body lies a-mouldering"

There's a new moon tonight.
I saw it in it's splendor.
And the trees, their branches are bare now,
Make lace-like patterns against it's face
As if they would hold it for a minute if they could.
The shadow of a rope still swings at Harper's Ferry.
It's frayed and grey. Swing softly.
Swinging shadows of grey tattered ropes
Can make great noises.

Yesterday, a father stood at the edge of the swamp
In the greyness of dawn crying, "Absolam! Absolam!"
Cut down your son.
Let the new moon make shadows of softness
Along the woods where the deer feed
And the grouse perch in the hemlocks.

The Indians will trade their reservation for tradition.
They will do the rain dance for the tourist.
There are red cliffs and a river
That is dry until the snows melt
And then rages hard by the red cliffs.
The coyote has great savvy.
Toward morning he will howl,
And the desert and the red cliffs
Will echo to the savvy of the coyote

Bare branches make a strange pattern
As if to hold the moon.
The coyote knows his own savvy.
Morning will come,
And the Indian can do a rain dance.
The shadow of a rope will swing forever.

God came
To my party,
And we had
No games to play
As roaring trains
Drown out the sound
Of a favorite song.
And the sun
    Went down
On my hopes
    Of understanding.

My good friend, the one you seek,
Her name in prayer I often speak,
Asking Him who rules the roost
To give her frame a little boost
And get her home just once on time
In happy mood and frame of mind
That she might share, at least in part,
A sample of my culinary art.

I know the sun, it's ways profound.
But there's a table to be found
That tells exactly when it will
Light the top of yonder hill.
The stars I know. With accuracy I
Can tell you when they leave the sky.
But with a wife there is no reason.
I can only hope she'll be home this season.

For Linda

I wonder why the small glimpse of childhood
Comes to be tamed
Into the alcatraz
Of adulthood.

I wonder why the earth
Should never quake
At the sound
Of every one-thousand butterfly sneezes.

I wonder why the instance of day,
Becoming confused
With the eternity of night,
Is defined as existence.

I wonder why life
Is fluid,
Insistent upon taking the shape
Of it's container.

And now that the light is near,
I wonder
What perfect prism might split the fear
And spill all my wonderings
Inside a single tear.

Cowslip and Cowlilly I thought the same
Yellow flower with two like names.
Now, late in life and in a book,
I learn the lily by the brook
Is Cowlilly, not to be confused
With Virginia Cowslip in the woods.

The Great White Hope

Just beyond the tenement slums
Of Washington's Massachusetts Avenue
Sprouts all the majesty
Of the nation's capitol.

Graceful winding pavement drives
Direct you to the home
Of the Great White Leader,
Residing in his Great White House.

And yet, reflecting lights sparkle
While my figure stands blurred
In the pool of the Potomac,
Cooled by breezes
Sneaking through apple blossoms,
Surrounded by memorials and monuments,
Mere copies of the grandeur that was Rome.

The Little People

Hopes,
Fears,
Smiles,
Tears,
And short happy years;
These belong to the little people
Because only they are free
From all the grown up inhibition
That has trapped us.

Only the little people
Have seen me clear enough
To memorize my ways,
Earning the right to laugh at me
Because together we are not afraid,
And they have become;
The purest happiness I have known.

Tiny minds,
Sensing hurt and happy
    deeper . . .
Than big people.
And a tear or two
That lasts only long enough
To make a path on a dirty face,
Because your grown up hand
Works miracles
As tears of fear
Become toys of joy
In the eyes of the little people.
And I am jealous,
Because I no longer have growing pains
To remind me of the little people inside.

RYE WHISKEY

Rye Whiskey — Rye Whiskey,
My friend and my foe.
Rye Whiskey — Rye Whiskey,
It's the one thing I know!

Old Eben Flood may have walked all alone,
But he had a good jug and was headed for home.
I think it was great that he stopped on a hill
And took a good swig from the juice of the still.

Rye Whiskey — Rye Whiskey,
With some bonnie lass
To be drinking and whoring!
But those days are past.

I still drink Rye Whiskey alone, and it's straight.
Walk with a cane and look so sedate.
Joined the Temperance Union. Put my name on the pledge.
And just drink that Whiskey when my nerves are on edge.

Brooklyn Before

The kid up the street was chasing me.
I wasn't even afraid in those days
When Pez dispensers were status symbols,
And the big people were never important
Because they couldn't wear sneakers
And ride three wheelers
Up Madison Street.

Remember the day I fell off the slide.
I guess I cried.
I hit my head.
I always hit my head.
My mother took me down to the 5 & 10,
And it made the hurt go away.
Maybe I should go to the 5 & 10 again.

I would, but my three wheeler
Would never make it.
I could stop at the water fountain,
But it has become too small,
Or I have grown
And remember I was never supposed to cross alone.
But still, there was never anyone to cross with.

I always had to call my mother
So she could see that it was safe
For me to cross.
But I had to yell so loud
That it hurt.
One day I crossed alone anyway.
I made it o.k.
And it hurt someone else.

But as things do change
We went away,
And a whole lot of the kid
Got left behind.
And it hurts
Because I just skinned my knee
On the memory.

Grandma died.
I planted an acre of pine,
And Philip was born.
All three events in that order to my family
Within a week of April sun and rain,
Feeling a sweet pain of remembrance
At having known she who was Mother to my wife,
And seeing the tiny pine trees shoulder
Their way into a nest of last year's leaves,
Pushing their tiny feet in the loam
Of other Summer's decaying life.

14841 Elderwood

Like a motionless pond,
I can lie here
Under the stars
And think of
My old address.

TO A TOAD

Wearing a belchy look,
Spring's little brother
Has slounched himself
Into a puddle of sunlight.
Immune to all,
Except the awakening warmth
That touches his back,
He squints one eye at me
As if he dares to ask,
"Brother, why didn't you sleep last night?"

Man has
Unfurled a flag, Minted a coin,
Named a God, Sensed the divine,
Built a temple, a pyramid, a bridge,
Sailed a boat through the unknown,
Crossed the ridge of space,
Walked on the moon,
Saw many civilizations fade away,
Threw a pinch of dirt saying dust to dust,
Counted the bones of a dinosaur,
And saw the red rust of a landing craft
On an island shore.

Christmas 1971

Amidst
  The bells
  Of Silent Night
  I experience one
  Again,
  Too silent,
Because
  Hard hats
  And plastic people
  Have skimmed the surface
  Of all I can give,
  And in questioning,
  All I have refused.
I still remain
  Liquid
  In the ice chest
  Of humanity.

In this harvest of leaves
Little sense I can find,
And the ones that I rake
Are mostly not mine,
But come with a wind
From a neighbor who grows
A shade for his house
And a multch for my rose
That's mine for the harvest.
It's a harvest — no more —
That's hardly worth keeping
If for free I could store.

Bryan Keith Padgett — October 6, 1972

Sometime Friday morning
The clock no longer read
1   2   3   4.
Somewhere between
The end of September
And the beginning of October
A clock stopped,
And time read
Something like
4   2   1   3
Because Dr. Seuss
Doesn't write books
About little boys
With unfinished paintings.

On some unborn evening I'll stand
While darkness fades out field and day
To call your name.
The hills will hear me
Calling, calling, calling
And send back muted echoes of "Away".

My lonesome cry will ring out
While the heavens become spangled
With a silvered starlight dew.
And an owl, tired from his night of hunting,
Will reveille the dawn with
"Who — who — who".

Kite String Isn't Strong Enough

You were happy
  Flying your kite alone
  All of the time.
I was happy
  Flying my kite and being alone
  Most of the time.
But yours would always glide
    steadily and confidently,
And mine would take one nose dive
    after another.
So believe me when I say:
I never meant to get in your way —
But somehow your kite string
Got tangled with mine,
And they both came down together.

The Villa

Of the good
A few things are accountable;
The possibility of a continuation
Only whispering now,
>*Like sunny afternoons*
>*With nothing trivial to do*
>*But let the sun*
>*Comfort you,*
>*And melt the inhibitions*
>*That keep you*
>*So very far from me,*
>*And . . .*
A tiny blade of grass
(More significant than most people)
>*That captures your concentration*
>*For an instant*
>*Taking your mind*
>*Down to simplicity,*
>*Or is it up,*
>*And . . .*
Good was you and me
For one time cherished
>*That will fade away*
>*Leaving me alone again*
>*With another*
>*Golden rhyme*
>*For all time.*

By a grey house with tall uncut grass
The summer moved, endless as time,
By an unpainted house grey with age
While August reached to me with open arms.
I spread a wide blade of fresh grass
Between my thumbs to make a whistle,
One shrill note on a grass blade to signal,
One sharp sound to tell a soft murmuring August
I was there standing alone by an unpainted house.
The shrill note came and there was a long silence.
The locusts took up my song,
Pushing it out beyond the fields to the woods,
And only I alone surrounded by tall grass
And a grey house with summer like cobwebs hanging
    from rafters.

I was so afraid
    Of being in winter
That I memorized
    A hot summer day
And a candy bar melted
    In my pocket.

FALL PLANTING

I planted a seed of doubt
Where little had ever grown.
I gave a thought that wasn't mine
To give or even own.
I'll never know if it grew or not
And admit I do not care.
At least I planted some thing
And left it sprouting there.

Bourbon Street

No parking,
An assortment
Of drunken tourists
And pushers
Leave me
With a feeling
That I got a hamburger
When I expected a steak.

This day lingers in my mind
As something that happened years ago.
I saw some clouds that drifted low along the hill,
And my heart filled with quietness
While I searched for thought or memory
To link it with yesterday.
It wasn't there.
But this day lingers in my mind.

Evening sky and lake had met
In a sheen of grey I'll not forget.
There were gulls, and there were boats
That seemed to fly and seemed to float.
But from the hill above there was no way
To separate the sky and bay.

September 4, 1971
Petoskey, Michigan

Other Worlds

Shifting sands
Are beginning to make
Patterns on my beach
Unlike sand castles and mermaids
Of days spent in happiness,

The sandcrabs are down there
Hiding from our world.
Much smarter than we,
They are
Taking comfort
Beyond awareness,
Drinking sunlight
Through saltwater.

Wandering around
Short times,
Many towns,
Instills in me
A fear
That's bringing on
A tear,
Like remembering
When there were
Notes on the floor
And three locks on the door
With time for a beer
And the end of a year.

I am leaving this world
A quarter of a pound at a time.
Each day I stand on scales
To match calories against pounds.
Some day, when that last bit
Of gristle and bone wastes away,
And those last few
Unhoused, unwanted, and unused calories
Fall to the ground,
My naked soul,
Answering only to the name of Maxwell,
Shall walk through and over
Bull thistles and broken bottles
Without pain.

June 1971

While looking for reasons
To live,
I tripped over
A few regrets,
Side tracked a few friends,
Wrote down only the important things,
And fell in love.